# So, You Want to Be

# A Coach

## Demystifying the Coaching Process

Written by Master Coach and Leading NLP Trainer
### Dr. Heidi Heron PsyD

*Published By:*

Worldwide Institutes of NLP
Level 7, 99 York Street
Sydney NSW 2000
Australia

**Websites:**

www.nlpworldwide.com
www.Coachtraining.co
www.anywherenlp.com

**Email:**
info@nlpworldwide.com

*Since 1994, The Worldwide Institutes of NLP has been providing NLP training around the globe – we have trained thousands of students in more than 12 countries.*

*Your Principal NLP Trainers, Dr. Heidi Heron PsyD, and Laureli Blyth, are not only Master Trainers of NLP, they also run their own private practices. They've successfully worked with thousands of people from individuals, teams, families, couples, leaders, groups to companies using NLP.*

*Both Laureli and Dr. Heidi are a part of the NLP Leadership Summit, made up of 120 of the world's leading trainers that meets every 2 years to Mastermind the ongoing development of NLP. Laureli and Dr. Heidi are Trainer Members and Clinical Professional Members with the Australian Board of NLP and both are Clinical Supervisors.*

# CONTENTS

# SO, YOU WANT TO BE A COACH?

Since 2016, Coaching has been one of the most sought-after skills to learn and the Coaching profession is on the rise.

If you have downloaded this book, I'm going to make a guess – either you are a Coach already and you're looking for some additional or proper accreditation, you work in Human Resources (or similar) and adding Coaching skills will be great for your skillset or you are playing with the idea of becoming a Coach – life Coach, business Coach, executive Coach, health Coach, etc.

Regardless of your why – you are in the right place. While I will be focusing on becoming a Coach, this book will be relevant for all of your questions. And, I know you have questions; you see, I've been training Coaches for nearly two decades – before the term for what we were doing officially became *Coaching*. I've talked to people during every aspect of becoming a Coach – even to people who decide not to pursue Coaching while they are in the middle of their training. I know you've got questions, and I want to provide you answers.

I believe it's also important for you to know that the modality that I use to Coach and train is Neuro Linguistic Programming (NLP). Most Coach training programs nowadays include aspects of NLP, but I have never felt that this light NLP touch was sufficient. I highly recommend that you complete both an NLP Practitioner and Master Practitioner training which also includes Coaching. More specifically (and transparently), I want to meet you in my training room someday soon and be the one who guides you on your journey to an exciting new career. Your skills as a Coach will expand exponentially with the growth you achieve in our practical NLP courses and will set you up for Coaching success.

I'd rather tell you this upfront, because you are going to hear a lot about my NLP Coach training in this book and integrity is one of my highest values. I want to be very transparent about my intentions behind this book, so you can get clear about yours.

With that in mind – here are my top 5 intentions for this book:

1.  Help you to know what Coaching is *and* what it is not
2.  Help you to figure out what the *business* of Coaching is all about
3.  Help you to find out if you really want to pursue a Coaching qualification
4.  Help you to know more about NLP as a Coaching modality
5.  Help you know the steps to take to become a Coach.

Regardless if you take up my invitation or not – with this book you will be better armed at making decisions for you that will set you up for success. After all, there are a lot of choices to be made when you decide to become a Coach.

A decision that will come sooner than later – is which Coach training to choose; and there are a lot to choose from! I'll be providing you with a list of questions to ask to potential trainers – this is not a decision to be taken lightly. The closest in distance, the cheapest in price or the shortest in duration are possibly none of the criteria you even want to consider when making this choice. But, more about that later.

I want to make sure you have your wits about you and your ducks in a row when making this decision, because it is an important one. Even simply the choice of "Do I want to go down the path of becoming a Coach", is important. I'll be very clear and upfront when I tell you, like any business – it's a business which requires your dedication, determination and persistence to make it a success. It can be a challenging, rewarding and fun business! The fun part is working with clients. And yes, sometimes it is challenging and less fun, but that's when you're growing. But then there is the rest of the activities – Marketing (websites, brochures, intriguing content, enticers), sales (conversations about your value, how you can help, your experience, maybe proposal writing, negotiating, managing resistance, objections or discount requests), your schedule, your time management, and your business finances (your income, expenses and taxation), managing it all - balancing the income (or in the beginning, your outcome until there is income!). We will discuss all of this so you can pursue this idea of becoming a Coach with your eyes wide open.

First, let me tell you a little about me.

Hi, I'm Dr. Heidi Heron. I started studying NLP in 1997. I was working in Human Resources where I learned about the communication and personal growth aspects of NLP and I wanted to know more. That is when I completed my Level 1, NLP Practitioner Certification training; and I was hooked!

My conversations after that training were richer, I was more focused, I was able to ask better questions and gain more clarity and I started to see my world in a different way. I now saw challenges as learning opportunities, failures as opportunities for growth, moments of being stuck as choices to either sit there or jump up. I was becoming more in charge of my mind, my emotions and my choices. I was empowering myself and it felt great! Soon after, I completed the Level 2 NLP Master Practitioner Certification training, and that's when my world began to transform.

I was using my conversational NLP skills more and more at work and in my daily life. I was starting to help others using the NLP tools to change their thought patterns, blocks and behaviours. During some evenings and weekends, I began to use NLP as a Coach/Therapist – I was helping a few people each week with NLP to get out of their own way and live the life they wanted. I began running some workshops at work that were NLP-based – and I knew that I needed to make a change.

Let me back up a minute – the reason I went into HR in the first place - honestly, it was where I could most easily get a job after finishing my University degrees.

I'm from Colorado in the USA, but you'll now find me living in Sydney, Australia – where I've been for the majority of the past 30 years. However, I did go to University in Colorado where I studied Communication and Psychology. Oddly, I didn't  learn much at all about how to help people, or communicate better or even find a suitable career path once I'd finished. My university studies in psychology were all about theories, statistics and research. I knew for sure I did not want to go down the traditional psychology or counselling road. So, Human Resources it was! But there was a lot less Human involved and a lot more Resources.

So, when I started to help people (and I mean really help people!) I knew that there was something more and real to this. Not only was I genuinely helping people using these NLP skills, but my heart would sing when I got the opportunity to do so. So, in 2000, I quit my real job and started my own NLP Coaching Practice. At that time I called myself a *Therapist.* If I could do the whole "quit my job" thing over again, I would do it differently and please allow me to share this with you later on. But suffice to say, I made it happen! I followed my heart and my gut, trusted my head brain to persevere and think outside the box – and stayed on my path to success.

At that same time, I teamed-up with Laureli Blyth as a co-Trainer. She had started the Australasian Institutes of NLP in 1996 (now known as The Worldwide Institutes of NLP), and was ready for an apprentice trainer. So, while most of my time was spent building my Coaching business (old school, no websites, no Facebook or other social media), and developing my skills as a Coach. Back then, there wasn't specific Coach training – it was all trial and error. Coaching was *becoming* a thing, but it wasn't there yet. The market was still in its infancy. Consumers were unsure of what to make of it and that's if they'd even heard of it at all.

It wasn't easy. The first 5 years of my Coaching business was hard. I won't lie or sugar coat it, I think that's important for you to know! I racked up thousands of dollars in credit card debt, ended up getting a part time job to pay bills and learned a lot about marketing – possibly more about what *didn't* work – which meant wasted time and money. Luckily, I get to now share this with my students and save them both time and money!

I connected, collaborated, created and found my way into the lives of many clients – and I asked for referrals, and they came! I found that the best *thank you,* validation and proof of my impact upon people was their referral – whereby they trusted me to help someone that was important to them. Today, 80% of my Coaching business are referrals.

While I was building my Coaching practice, I was also training NLP with Laureli and setting up my own groups and trainings to offer more services. I ran a Time Management, Leadership, Managing for New Managers, Communication Skills training and more. I knew that diversifying my business somewhat was going to be important. I also am quite technically savvy and knew the internet was going to be important for business and education in the future.

So, to keep my mind active and focused, I completed my master's degree in Adult Education with an emphasis on Online Learning. Talk about foresight! Those skills have come in so extremely handy over the past decade as online learning continues to grow and change.

I then embarked on more Coach Training. From simple Coach Training to Meta Coaching Bootcamp, I started to gain more skills and understanding. Really, an understanding that what I was doing with my clients was often better than the training I was attending. I found most of the Coach Training I attended was very light on skills to help people. I learned how to connect with clients, how to ask questions about what they want, how to create an accountability plan and motivate my client to move forward and conversationally challenge them when needed. I didn't learn any tools to help clear beliefs, remove un-resourceful blocks or patterns that get in people's way. In fact, the majority of the time I was taught to "refer on" to a therapist when blocks come up for Coaching clients.

**Key learning from Coach Training:** traditional Coaching is focused on the *desired state.*

In around 2008, with a successful Coaching Practice and Training business, I was ready for my next challenge and started to work on my Doctorate in Clinical Psychology. I knew that my original roots in psychology had left me wanting for more, and I was curious to know if having even more formal study was going to help me to be a better Coach. During my doctoral work, I had classroom-based training with various assignments, and a research thesis. I learned a lot during the entire program, and my thesis is based on "Resilience as q Preventative and Curative tool for Trauma". I loved that tedious project (*loved* might be a bit strong! I loved when I was done with it!).

Through that adventure, I found the answer to my question – will more formal study in psychology help me to be a better Coach. The answer. No.

In fact, had it not been for my NLP skills, I think I would be more harmful than helpful for my clients. You see, the majority of my studies taught me to diagnose psychological issues, to talk around where someone is, but not address what they want instead. I was not armed with any specific tools that allowed me to help people and I learned how to help people to cope or manage a diagnosis or situation in their life.

These are the exact reasons I didn't go into psychology in the first place.

**Key learning from psychology:** traditional psychology is focused on the *present state.*

So, what my formal studies DID do – it reaffirmed my understanding and belief that NLP is the must-have tool for all counsellors, psychotherapists and Coaches.

By this time (around 2010), Coaching was now a thing! So, my education also gave me more insight into what Coaching is and what it is not, where it fits, and how extremely beneficial NLP is to bridge the gap.

It was around this timeframe that I started to consolidate my learnings, the trainings that we offered and create something spectacular. What was born from this, is our NLP Coach Certification Training. I am extremely proud of this program – it contains Level 1 and 2 of NLP plus specific Coaching elements and enough assignments, assessments and feedback to help our students develop exceptional Coaching skills. I'm also proud to tell you, our NLP Coach Certification training is an Accredited Coach Training Program (ACTP), with the International Coach Federation (ICF). This is the highest accolade we could ever achieve. The ICF is the premier global body for accrediting Coaches. Their standards are high, and their accreditation and credentials weigh heavily in many people's decision strategy. After all, if you want to be the best, you have to train with the best.

I am what some people may consider to be a *high achiever*. It's how I'm programmed. I don't need anything to be perfect, but I want to do my best, and help others to do theirs. All of the training I completed, investigated and looked at was all missing something. And, it was my mission to build that bridge and create one of the most comprehensive and robust Coach Training programs available.

During all of this, I had to formalise my own studies and credentials. So, with over 4000 Coaching hours I now hold Master Certified Coach (MCC) with the ICF, Level 4 membership with the Australian Counsellors Association, Clinical and Trainer Membership with the Australian NLP Association as well as my Doctorate in Clinical Psychology.

Since 2014, I have been listed with a group called Global Guru's on their Top 30 NLP Professionals in the World, as I write this I currently sit at #5 on that list, and #17 on the Top 30 Coaches in the World – the same list as Tony Robbins (who is currently at #8).

While these lists don't really mean anything in the long run, what it means to me is that I do good work. Both as a Trainer and Coach. It means that the work I do is seen, respected and sought after.

Currently, my Coaching practice time is in high demand. Because of the other demands on my time, I am limited to working with just 10-12 clients per week, and most often, there is a 3-4 week waiting time to see me. I know if I focused only on Coaching, I could work with 30-40 clients per week.

But, for now, my focus is on training Coaches. I know that my impact on the world will be a greater one by training others to do what I do, to the degree that I do it. That is my purpose, passion and contribution to the Coaching world.

I welcome you to the journey.

# CHAPTER 1

# A LOOK AT COACHING

At its core, Coaching is a dynamic conversation with another person, or group of people that acts as a sounding board, mirror, challenger, supporter and celebrator. People may seek a Coach to be an accountability partner, to help them create an action plan, to address limitations or fears or even have an impartial person to brainstorm with. A Coach has the ability to look at a person's life and challenges from an outside perspective – there isn't emotion or agenda from the Coach, so the client can be fully supported in his or her desires.

As I mentioned before, the benefit of an NLP Coach over a traditional Coach is the depth and breadth of how you can assist your clients. An NLP Coach has a remarkable job of helping others to navigate through their life – highlighting potential pitfalls, addressing blocks and interferences for success and helping to build resources that are needed to achieve the clients' desires.

You will learn a simple formula called the **NLP Formula** for working with clients. As a Coach, you will be interested in not only what the client desires for their future – but where they are now and how they got there. An NLP Coach will presuppose that the client has everything they need to achieve their desires and they simply need some help accessing beliefs, attitudes, behaviours and other necessary resources; so, as a Coach you will use various NLP tools to access and build resources with your client. Additionally, and somewhat unique to NLP Coaching, you will help to identify any blocks, limitations or barriers to success and help to change these patterns at an unconscious level.

What we often find is that emotions like fear, anxiety, lack of self-belief, low confidence, low self-esteem, etc., and patterns like perfectionism, procrastination, self-sabotage, negative thinking, etc often hold people back from achieving what they want, sometimes from even trying to achieve their desires. Luckily, NLP contains tools and exercises that will help you to not only identify and address these patterns but change and eliminate them if that is the want of the client.

As a Coach, you have the amazing job to help people figure out what they want and how to achieve it; but you don't need any answers at all. The answers come from your client. What you will need are powerful questions and an assortment of tools to help you help your client in the best way possible.

Some of the topics people might bring to Coaching include (but is not limited to):

- Starting/getting a new job
- Project work
- Increasing effectiveness
- Dealing with overwhelm and busy-ness
- Effective leadership/management
- Identifying and overcoming barriers
- Improving communication skills
- Becoming a team player
- Staying focused and motivated
- Career exploration
- Improving health and well-being
- Increasing confidence and self-belief
- Creating more self-awareness
- Accountability
- Setting boundaries
- Preparing for conflict
- Taking things less personally
- Dealing with the imposter syndrome
- Feeling in control
- Releasing negative emotions
- Transforming limiting beliefs
- Improving relationships
- Building inner strength
- Handling grief and change
- Stress management and reduction
- Find direction

- Discovering/re-discovering passion
- Creating more balance in life
- Reducing negative self-talk
- Values alignment
- Goal setting
- Increasing productivity
- Creating new or eliminating habits
- Increasing proactive-ness
- Manage transition
- To have a sounding board
- Increase security
- Have more fun and happiness in life
- Leave a legacy

With all of this being said, becoming a Coach and helping people is the ultimate in job satisfaction! Sometimes I work with people who have been stuck for years. Then finally they get help to figure out what they want, help to release the past and assistance to grab the future with both hands and the confidence to get there. Being able to *help people to live their best life* is one of the best things about this job. Besides that, it offers a great deal of flexibility and a lot of variety – there has not been one of my days that has been the same as another!

## WHAT COACHING IS NOT

Sometimes people call themselves a Coach, but they are not doing Coaching. One key identifier is this – **who has the answers and advice?**

If the answer is the Coach. You are not Coaching. You are teaching, advising, consulting or mentoring.

A Coach does not provide answers or advice, this comes from the client.

If you have a weight loss program that is very structured with step by step instructions and a plan to follow and you "Coach" your clients through the process, it is more likely that you are mentoring. However, if you have conversations that are addressing their particular needs, emotions, beliefs, etc, in a way that helps to empower, upskill and enhance the overall wholeness of your client, then you are Coaching.

If you are giving career advice, advising how to move into a new line of work or what study is required to progress, you are more likely in the role of advisor or consultant. If, however, you are discussing the values, strengths and dreams of a client and helping them to create their own plan, you may be in a Coaching role.

Bottom line, who drives the Coaching conversation?

The International Coaching Federation (ICF), defines Coaching in the following way:

> *Coaching is partnering with clients in a thought-provoking and creative process that inspires them to maximize their personal and professional potential.*

# TYPES OF COACHING

At the end of the day, Coaching is about helping another person to move from where they are now, to where they want to be. Along the way, a skilled Coach will have tools to ask questions, gather information, identify interferences and resources needed, while having the tools and skills to remove/transform those interferences and help build and access resources.

Traditionally, Coaching has been categorised into difference *types* of Coaching. But some Coaches work across the board with whatever their clients want to work on. Regardless of the type of Coaching, the structure of Coaching remains largely the same. Let's take a general look at the different types of Coaching.

## LIFE COACHING

A Life Coach works mainly with individuals on personal goals and issues. This might include emotions, relationships, finding one's purpose, dealing with behaviours, beliefs and thoughts that stand in the way, or even working toward a personal goal.

## BUSINESS COACHING

A Business Coach works either with a businessperson or within a business. The topics a client may bring could be about starting or expanding a business, improving communication, releasing a personal belief or habit, building more confidence, improving leadership skills or even moving toward a business goal.

Working within a business, as a Coach, may entail team or group Coaching about a goal, leadership skills, shared values or managing change.

## EXECUTIVE COACHING

An Executive Coach may primarily work with C-Suite individuals, but the topics may be very similar to Life or Business Coaching. More and more, organisations are engaging ICF credentialed Coaches to work with their executive team – from personal experience, the topics I help people with fall mainly into the categories or balance, stress and improving confidence.

## TRANSITION COACH

A Transition Coach works with people who are going through a transition. Change is one of the biggest stressors in life, and having a Coach to assist with emotional challenges, creating a new direction and dealing with grief from loss is useful. This may include changes in relationship, career, family, home, retirement or anything else that creates possible stress from change.

## WELLNESS/HEALTH COACH

A Wellness/Health Coach assists their clients primarily with physical and mental wellbeing. This may include fitness, nutrition, weight loss, and overall health. Often, this type of Coach specialises in another aspect that they bring into Coaching. Remember, a Coach doesn't give advice, so if you are giving advice around fitness, nutrition, behaviours, etc., then you are adding advisory and consulting skills into Coaching.

## CAREER COACH

A Career Coach helps people generally find and transition their career. This may mean identifying strengths, finding new career paths and working toward helping the client secure a new role. A Career Coach may assist clients with resumes, interview skills and bolstering confidence during a job search. Often, Career Coaches have additional training or HR experience.

## FINANCE COACH

A Finance Coach is often trained in other skills that may include financial planning or accounting. The aim of a Finance Coach is to help people address their beliefs and behaviours around financing to assist a savings or spending plan for an individual or business. If financial advice is given, a Finance Coach also holds a dual role as an advisor and consultant and should have adequate insurance to cover for this advice.

Of course, there are many types of Coaching, and you do not have to limit yourself to one type of Coaching. While many Coaches choose to niche or specialise – which, from a marketing standpoint makes a lot of sense, you don't have to. We have compiled some specialties you might want to consider:

| Executive/Business Coaching | Interpersonal Relationship Coaching |
| --- | --- |
| Corporate Coach | Marriage Coach |
| Executive/CEO Coach | Family Coach |
| Organisational development Coach | Romance Coach |
| | Team Coach |
| Leadership Coach | Love Coach |
| Culture change Coach | Divorce recovery Coach |

Sales Coach
Marketing Coach
Entrepreneur Coach
Networking Coach
Business Development Coach
Brand management Coach

Couples Coach
Intimacy Coach

### Life Stage/Lifestyle Coaching
Fresh start Coach
Generation X Coach
Baby boomer Coach
Millennial Coach
Retirement Coach
Lifestyle design Coach
Student Coach
Transition Coach
Sexuality Coach
Empty nesters Coach

### Success Coach
Motivation Coach
Goals/results Coach
Creativity Coach
Problem Solving Coach
Time management Coach
Strategic Coach
Attraction Coach
Financial/money Coach
Career Coach
Confidence Coach

### Quality of Life Coach
Nutrition/diet Coach
Exercise/fitness Coach
Recreation Coach
Wellness Coach

Makeover Coach
Stress reduction Coach
Energy Coach
Addiction Coach

# WHY DO PEOPLE HIRE A COACH?

The desire for people to hire a Coach is on the rise. In the past 10 years, people have gained more of an understanding that they can do better when they have help, and they are more open to seeking help. Although there are parallels of a Coach and a Therapist, there seem to still be a lot of stigmas about seeing a Therapist. Most people these days are more likely to seek the assistance of a Coach versus a Therapist.

The reasons people choose to work with a Coach are as varied as the topics we can think of. Some people seek out and pay for a Coach on their own whilst others are provided a Coach through the workplace. My personal preference is when someone has sought a Coach on their own, because there often is more ownership and responsibility. I even find sometimes with Business and Executive Coaching, even when the client has chosen to work with a Coach – if the business weren't paying for it, the client may not embark on the Coaching. In either case, I vet my clients well to make sure they want to work with me, and they personally have a vested interest in their outcomes. After all, as a Coach, I am just a facilitator - any change that occurs is up to the client.

Taking a big picture view, here are a few reasons why people will seek the assistance of a Coach:

**To set better goals** – often people have limiting thoughts about what they can do and what they want. A Coach is useful to help a client set a Well-Formed Outcome, which is a robust goal with steps and evidence of reaching this goal.

**To reach their goals** - having a goal is the first step, achieving it is the next. A Coach can help point out roadblocks, identify interferences and help the client to build the needed resources to realise their goal. Sometimes as a Coach you will be an accountability partner, a motivator and a constant support for your client to get to where they desire.

**To make significant changes** – being able to have someone in your corner when significant changes arise is a very useful strategy. As a Coach, you may be the sounding board, advocate and support mechanism for your client as they make choice, navigate change and forge a new road into their future.

**To create and live their best life** – we are all doing the best we can with what we have available in this moment. Sometimes, a Coach is needed to unleash even more potential, create plans, tap into purpose and help our clients to realise their best life. This may entail identifying and clearing limiting patterns, setting goals and taking action on steps to attaining the life they want.

**To get ahead professionally** – often people will seek the support of a Coach to gain new skills or change behaviours. This may mean that you are using your NLP skills to create new behaviours or clear unresourceful patterns. It may also mean that you are putting on your hat of an educator and sharing new capabilities of communication, building rapport and leadership.

**To have an accountability partner** – who are you accountable to? While some people are able to be self-motivated and accountable to themselves, other people need an external party to be accountable to; and often they either don't have that person, or that person is too close to the situation. Therefore, having a Coach serving as an accountability partner is a great way to make progress, stay motivated and pave a solid pathway to the attainment of goals.

**To get out of their own way** – people are often their own worst enemy. Working with a skilled Coach who can help a person get out of their own way can be extremely beneficial. This may entail identifying and clearing self-sabotaging thoughts, behaviours and beliefs; allowing your client to have more choice, control and responsibility for their life.

**To transform limiting beliefs** – based on my Coaching experience, 85-90% of why we do what we do comes down to beliefs, often limiting beliefs that hold us back. As an NLP Coach, you will have skills to help identify and transform these beliefs in a very short timeframe. This is a game changer when it comes to human evolution.

**To improve their behaviours and habits** – we all have behaviours and habits that we would like to change, but most of us don't know how to make these changes without big sacrifices of time and energy. Enter an NLP Coach. You will have the skills and tools to work with a person's unconscious programming to help change and improve the behaviours and habits with your clients.

**To improve their relationships with others** – sometimes relationships suffer because we either don't understand enough about another person, or we think what we are doing will work for someone else. As a Coach, you have the ability to help people learn about others and about themselves. Improving a person's knowledge and transform into being more respectful of what others need and want, therefore being able to improve relationships, be a better leader, parent, manager, friend, spouse and overall person.

**To simplify their life** – complexity comes in many forms – space, thought, behaviour and attitude. Sometimes a Coach is needed to help simplify life. This may mean decluttering life or their mind. Sometimes you will help perfectionists, control artists, over thinkers and 'negative Nelly's' take a simpler approach to life. As a Coach, helping your client to identify and create a simpler mode of operandi can lead to years of happiness!

**To create more balance** – many years ago, the adage was creating 'work/life balance', I think more and more people are realising this is simply just 'balance'. As a Coach, you are able to help demystify personal concepts, help realign behaviours and help your clients to reach more congruent states of balance in their lives.

**To reduce stress** – stress is still the number one killer in the world. As a Coach, you will be able to help pinpoint creators of stress, collapse anchors, help create new channels for stress and new strategies for handling stressful situations. From a productivity and long-term health perspective, there isn't much better than that!

**To strengthen their confidence and self-worth** – at some point in their lives, everyone needs a Confidence Coach. You will have so many tools to help your clients to create more personal confidence, self-worth, self-belief and even self-love. When a person possesses these resources, very little can stop them.

**To increase their income** – while you may not have a product or service that immediately helps your clients to increase their income, you will have many tools to help get their mindset and psychology aligned with an increase. So often, I find that the beliefs, values and attitudes toward money actually stop people from creating and having the wealth they want and desire. A Coach can help with this.

**To improve their health** – over the years I have worked with countless people to improve their health. This might mean creating new strategies to help motivate them to go to the gym, meditate or eat right. It also may mean assisting your client to align their desires and beliefs for weight loss or unwinding a disease from their mind and body. This may also mean helping people move through and from depression, anxiety, fears and other health limitations.

As a Coach, you can help people to do, change, create and enhance so many aspects of their life. I often find that a client will initially come to me for one reason and continue to work with me over time for a variety of others.

One of my favourite aspects of Coaching, specifically NLP Coaching, is that as a Coach you don't need to be the master of any issue or problem; that is your client's job. You just need to have the right questions and right tools to help your client to really know what they want, how to clear interferences holding them back and build resources that will help them to get to where they want to go.

Enter NLP.

# CHAPTER 2

# INTRODUCING NLP

**Neuro Linguistic Programming** is a grouping of concepts, methodology and skills to help you understand how the language of the mind creates the programs you run in life. The actual definition of NLP will vary from person to person, because depending on what you are using it for and who you are using it with, it is an adaptable and flexible tool.

What we'd like to do is take a few minutes to frame NLP as a Coaching and personal growth tool, because that is what it will be as you embark on learning this modality.

First, let's look at the basic descriptions of NLP:

> **Neuro** – the neuro of NLP deals with the mind and brain. However, not just the brain that sits in your head, we are interested in all the neurology within your being. Every cell, atom, chemical, hormone and neurological connection.

> **Linguistic** – the linguistic of NLP has to do with your senses. We are interested in the verbal and non-verbal aspects of anything you can be aware of - what you see, hear, taste, touch, smell and think.

> **Programming** – the programming part of NLP is the most important. You have programming (or patterning) about everything you do; your beliefs, behaviours, actions, thoughts, and moods are based on the programming that you have.

Possibly, the real order of NLP should be, LNP – linguistic, neuro, programming (it just doesn't sound as good!). Everything that goes on around you are taken up **linguistically** – every single thing you've ever seen, said, tasted, touch, smell, thought or felt is within your awareness. Automatically, what has come into your awareness connects with your **neurology,** based on the internal or external stimuli, your brain creates and secretes chemicals, hormones and neurotransmitters that instantly trigger your unconscious **programming** and you have a physical, mental or emotional reaction. Instantly.

Let's look at a simple example. There may be a certain way a person can say your name that triggers an emotion from you. Here's what is happening:

1.  You hear your name being said in a specific way (linguistic)

2.  Your brain automatically creates and secretes a chemical based on what you've heard (neuro)

3.  Your body immediately triggers an emotional reaction (programming)

So, NLP is understanding how the language of your mind creates the programs of your life. NLP also contains skills and knowledge that allows you to identify how the programs were created, how to enhance the programs that work well, how to change what doesn't work well to be able to create the programming you desire.

As you will learn, you can use NLP to better communicate with others by learning more about how they have been programmed to understand, behave and think; you can use NLP as a personal development tool to understand more about yourself, grow, change and align your programming; in business you can use NLP to better understand and use the psychology of others; for your own health you can use NLP to align the mind/body connection; and you can use the skills of NLP as  modality for helping others in all aspects of life as a Coach or Therapist.

Throughout this book, you will hear us talking a lot about the **conscious** and **unconscious** mind. The conscious mind is thought to make up only 10% of our mind – it is responsible for thinking, analysing, judging and reasoning. While you may think it is your conscious mind that is in charge of you because you may be so aware of its incessant chatter, this isn't the case. Your **unconscious mind** makes up the other 90% of your mind, also known as the subconscious or non-conscious mind, it is really this part of you that runs your body. It also stores your memories, creates your emotions, creates and transmits chemicals and is responsible for every part of your life.

It is your unconscious mind that we are interested in from an NLP perspective as this is the part of your mind responsible for storing and using your programs and patterns of emotion, thoughts, beliefs and behaviour. If you've ever tried to logic your way into health or happiness, you'll know that your conscious mind isn't responsible for such things. It is your unconscious mind that we use in NLP.

It was through studying and eventually modelling a few successful therapists in the 1970's, who were identifying a relationship between the unconscious mind and its ability to be programmed and reprogramed, that led to the development of NLP as we know it today. Specifically, Fritz Perls, a Gestalt therapist; Virginia Satir, a family therapist; and Dr. Milton Erickson, a hypnotherapist, all obtained exceptional results with their clients and used specific techniques that worked and communicated directly with the unconscious mind. As you are undoubtedly aware of the plasticity of our brains, these therapists understood and used this concept before the term neuroplasticity was even coined.

The three official founders of NLP are Richard Bandler, John Grinder and Frank Pucelik, plus there was a group of a dozen other specialists who were involved in the modelling and development of various concepts.

None of the core group were trained therapists, but they were curious enough to experiment with different concepts and learnings they gathered from Virginia, Frits and Milton to create what we know today as NLP.

One of Richard Bandler's definitions of NLP is "It's an attitude of curiosity and a methodology that leaves behind a trail of techniques".

The tools of NLP understandably have been incorporated into a lot of different fields including leadership, sales, management, education, parenting and of course Coaching. As I mentioned before, concepts of NLP are often now taught in more traditional Coach training programs. The vast difference with the NLP Coach Certification we provide is that we don't just touch upon NLP; NLP is the essential part of the program. You will be immersed in NLP – which is a pre-requisite to learning the Coaching tools.

# NLP PRESUPPOSITIONS

NLP is grounded in a variety of principles referred to as *Presuppositions* which set the foundation for the modality. These are more guidelines than rules, but they fit extremely well into client-centric Coaching. Let's take a look at a few:

- Everyone has all the resources they need to achieve their desired outcomes
- People work perfectly
- There is no failure, only feedback
- Every behaviour has a positive intention
- People are doing the best they can with the resources they have
- There are multiple ways of doing/seeing everything

From a Coaching standpoint, filtering through some of these NLP Presuppositions helps the client to believe, trust and honour their client; in turn, the client learns to do the same.

Sometimes with clients, I am simply filtering with Presuppositions and other times I am educating my clients. I am helping them to understand that they are doing the best they can right in this moment, and with Coaching, we have the ability to uncover more resources, clear limits and assist them to be more resourceful in the next moment. I am helping them to realise that they are not at all broken but working perfectly with how their current programming is set. With NLP, we can create new unconscious programming — to help that perfect programming work even better to help a person live the life they want.

I know that without the NLP Presuppositions, my Coaching would be missing something very elemental and foundational. And, my clients would often be missing an ingredient that goes with them long after our Coaching has finished.

# THE NLP FORMULA

I've briefly talked about the NLP Formula — but let me share a bit more about how NLP is used as a modality of Coaching.

In traditional Coaching, the focus is on what the client wants, we call this the **desired state**. In traditional counselling, the focus is on where the client is, we call this the **present state**. In NLP Coaching, which is a deliberate hybrid of Coaching and counselling, we require information and details about what the client wants, where the client is and how they got there.

As you learned before in the explanation of NLP, we are interested in the unconscious programming of our clients. Through a set of client intake questions, you will learn about the patterns of emotions, beliefs, thoughts, behaviours and habits that helps and hinders your client's success. Using this information, you'll then be able to identify your clients Interferences (those things that are barriers, blocks or limits to success), and the resources needed (for example, confidence, motivation, self-belief, etc.) to achieve their desired outcome.

You will then be able to apply various techniques you will learn in the certified NLP trainings that are designed to specifically clear these interferences and access resources. You will learn tools to help change beliefs, build confidence, create anchors, collapse anchors, clear traumatic events, create new behaviours, align values, change self-concept, boost self-worth, enhance identity and so much more!

The following is a diagram and listing of some of the NLP tools you will learn in the NLP trainings of the Coach Certification.

- Auditory Perspective
- Submodality Belief Change
- Change Personal History
- Changing Values
- Neurological Levels Alignment
- Sacred Journey
- Release Anxiety & Worry
- Submodality Changes
- Depleasuring Process
- Meta Stating Concepts

- Collapsing Anchors
- Communicating with Symptoms
- Meta Stating Troubling Emotions
- Foreground Background
- Neuro Repair Change
- State Management
- Unconscious Pattern Change
- Changing Strategies
- Visual Kinesthetic Dissociation
- Sleight of Mouth Patterns

- Meta Model
- Changing Meta Programs
- Reframing
- Metaphors
- Parts Integration
- Swish Pattern
- Meta Questions
- Tunneling
- Reimprinting
- Drop Down Through

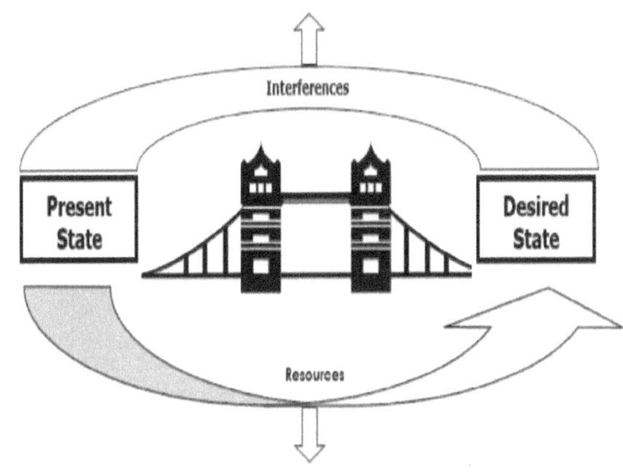


- Resource Anchor
- Sleight of Mouth Patterns
- Changing Timeline
- Eliciting Values
- Metaphors
- New Behaviour Generator
- Virus Protector
- Self Concept

- Circle of Excellence
- Disney Planning Process
- Chunking Up and Down
- Integrating Anchors
- Modelling
- Perceptual Positions
- Meta States
- Visual Perspective

- Meta Programs
- Mapping Meta Programs
- Meta Model
- Reframing
- Neurological Levels
- Prime Concerns
- Meta Questions
- Strategies

# CHAPTER 3

# THE JOY OF COACHING

Not only can you make a decent part-time or full-time living from being a Coach, it is a very rewarding career too. Being able to help people reach their goals, get out of their own way and live a better life is amazing, I hope you are as excited about this prospect as I am for you!

Part of my own journey and joy of working with people is the ability to truly help them. Over the years, I have assisted people overcome health issues, climb out of depression, get themselves unstuck, connect with others better, trust themselves, achieve goals – write books, start business, have babies and so many other things.

As I've mentioned, and will continue to mention – it is sometimes a challenging business, but the joy or helping outweighs all of the challenges combined.

My life will be forever improved because of the work I do. I feel that for a Coach to be excellent or extraordinary in the work they do, their first client is themselves. I have, and continue to apply my NLP and Coaching skills to my life. When I see blocks or interferences pop up, I address them. When I have a goal, I use my tools to create a well-formed outcome, a plan and steps to Coach myself to achieving my goal. And, when I am feeling angry, stuck, sad or frustrated, I use my skills to Coach myself in the best way possible; sometimes that means owning my emotion and moving through them.

It truly is a joy living authentically as a Coach. Not only do I have implied permission to live my best life, and I get to help others do the same, I make a pretty good living as a Coach. Over the years, I have worked with hundreds of client from around the world for thousands of hours of Coaching. Currently, I'm sitting at nearly 5000 hours of Coaching hours – it gives me great joy, pleasure and pride to have helped that many people; with more to come.

If I chose to, I could have a thriving business simply based on Coaching others, but I mix it up a bit with training, consulting and running the businesses – having these different layers is fun for me too. I know I'm a better trainer because I'm a great Coach! Each element of the work I do compliments the others.

I can imagine as life progresses, I will always work as a Coach – even in a part-time capacity. Right now, my focus is on training Coaches who want to help others, but my initial desire to assist and aid people in their transformation will always burn brightly for me.

I love watching the lightbulbs go on, hearing new beliefs take form and seeing a new and improved person walk out of my office after we've had a few sessions. The spirit of people around the world is the same – we all want to be happy, be loved and live our best lives. Sometimes *life* gets in the way and we need help. This is where a Coach can come in. This is where YOU can come in.

## HELPING OTHERS

I wanted to highlight a few clients that I've worked with to show you some of the impact NLP Coaching has, and the types of people you can help. For confidentiality purposes, I've changed the clients names and any irrelevant information to protect their identity.

### JOHNATHAN – 35 YEAR OLD MALE

I worked with Johnathan for a total of 6 sessions over a few months. His presenting issue was a lack of motivation, drive, enthusiasm or follow-through. He explained that he had been depressed, anxious and stuck for some time. Johnathan had a part-time job that provided him enough to pay a small rent and to buy food, but that was about it. His desired state was to feel again, to reconnect with himself and his motivation.

Through our initial discussions, I learned that Johnathan had been abandoned as a 3 day old baby and adopted by a family who had loved him, but he always felt lost and alone. He had an underlying belief that he wasn't good enough and would never amount to anything – therefore why try?

Together, we cleared a variety of self-limiting beliefs and boosted his confidence, self-worth and belief in himself and the future. This is an excerpt from an email exchange we had a few months after working together:

> *Thank you again for EVERYTHING! I still don't know how to adequately express my gratitude... If anything I'm feeling too normal.*
>
> *But I had a flick through Meet-Up and have already flagged several groups that I'd be interested in doing things with, way out of the box for me! Anyway, I'm looking forward to bounding across these stepping stones you helped me create in the near future, and am already looking forward to the next step in this new life!*

## NATALIE – 48 YEAR OLD FEMALE

Natalie has run her own business for the past 12 years, and came to see me because her sales were decreasing, her self-belief was going down and her internal critical voice was at an all-time-high. She had been doing the same thing for a very long time and didn't have the innovation, motivation or know-how to reinvent her company, and her self-talk was so negative she was stuck in a loop of sameness.

Over 8 months we worked together, initially every week and eventually just once per month. Using a process called the Disney Planning Process we realigned her to her business and her dream for the business and we created a plan. Within this we identified old patterns of emotion and beliefs popping up and transformed these using NLP. With monthly accountability Coaching, Natalie was able to convert her business into a powerhouse again – boosting sales and self-belief.

It was a pleasure to be a part of her journey, to help her see the possibilities and to spark her innovation to create her business again how she wanted it.

## ANTHONY – 17 YEAR OLD MALE

Anthony was sent to see me by his parents. He presented with what could have been diagnosed with bi-polar disorder, extreme mood swings from out of the blue. He teetered between suicidal depression and reckless manic states, and felt extremely out of control in all aspects of his emotions.

We worked together for a total of 6 sessions, the first simply exploring how life had been and what he wanted. There was a lot of apprehension to create a change because he was afraid of again falling into depression and suicidal thoughts. But, together, I helped him to find a desired state that he hoped would be manageable and simple to live with.

Possibly one of the most profound aspects of working with Anthony was in our third session together when he came to a realisation that he had more choice over his emotions than he thought he ever did. With this new understanding came empowerment and self-belief that he could live a better life, he simply needed to decide what he wanted.

We identified a variety of challenges and beliefs we needed to work on and change, namely – he needed to be liked and didn't like conflict of any kind. If he perceived either of these, this would spiral him downward – and when he was able to be jovial, make people laugh and be the life of the party, upward he would go.

Over the time we worked together, Anthony created more balance in his emotions as well as a stronger sense of confidence and self-belief. He no longer needed to be liked and found conflict to be a natural part of life, even if it wasn't always comfortable.

The following is an excerpt from an email exchange with Anthony's father:

> *We have certainly noticed a lot more stability and calm in Anthony, so something is definitely working in his assessment, judgement and action response to things in his life! To be honest I don't think I have even seen him 'down' in recent weeks including through a recent family incident. Thank you so much for your help!*

## LESLIE – 56 YEAR OLD WOMAN

Leslie is a professional woman who has been working with the same company for over twenty years, more recently in a new male dominated department. We worked together for 6 sessions working on her self-belief, confidence and strength to continue to do good work and stand up for herself and her skills.

Shortly after moving into her new role she began to be bullied in the workplace by her manager and colleagues. She had reported this to her superiors, but nothing had changed. She was worried they were trying to push her out, and this was impacting on her productivity, confidence and belief.

In our sessions together, we uncovered a desire to prove herself and do her best – while at the same time feeling ridiculed and belittled by men.

We were able to change some fundamental beliefs Leslie had about her skills, working with men, expectations of others and being judged.

She came to realise that the bullying she was experiencing, although not appropriate, was possibly not even bullying – it was simply not the female nurturing she was used to and she had been taking it very personally based on her past experiences and beliefs about men and male work ethic. Together, we were able to boost her resourcefulness, help her regain her personal power and find her confidence once again.

About 4 months after working together she emailed me to tell me about an award she had received at work for her efforts, teamwork and reliability.

My desire and intention with Coaching is to leave the world a better place. As a Coach, I have the honour to walk with people in their lives and help them to live their best life. This might be improving an aspect of communication, helping them create a pathway for their business or being able to better manage their emotions.

I could continue to give you example after example of peoples lives that I have touched as a Coach, but I would rather inspire and help you to become a Coach to also help people. The art of Coaching is truly a rewarding skill to have!

# WORK/LIFE BALANCE

As you will learn through this book, the business of Coaching isn't always an easy one – and isn't a quick 6 figure income type of job for many people; but the balance that you can have in life when you do it right is amazing.

As a Coach, you have options of working from home, remotely, from a serviced office, co-working space or office of your own or shared with others. Your working hours are up to you too! I know many Coaches who only see clients in the evenings, or on weekends or during the day.

If you have a family to balance, or another source of income, Coaching allows you total flexibility.

If you are looking to set up your own business, this also means being your own boss! And what a great boss you will be, won't you? While this can sometimes be a downside with no one to be accountable to, if you are motivated by a challenge then you will love being your own boss. You set your hours, work days and outcomes. The wins of your company come down to you and the feeling of creating a successful business that helps others is a total pleasure to run.

Currently, I run my Coaching practice just two days per week. I see client on just Tuesdays and Thursdays, both in my office and online. I limit my clients to just 5 per day, or 10 per week and the income I am earning is sustainable and enough for me to live on if I were to do only Coaching. I however, also train, develop Coaches and do a few other things, so my days are extremely varied. As a new Coach, you may be working more hours to build your practice, your skills and your clients – but overtime this will even out and you can have even more flexibility of when and how you work.

# VARIETY

If you are like many Coaches, you thrive on variety and difference. While the overall job of Coaching has the same structure, every single day you are working with clients will be different. With NLP Coaching specifically, there is not a set or standard process to Coaching – every person you meet will have their own stories, interferences, goals, history and model of the world.

As a Coach, you have the beautiful job of getting to know different people and helping them to access the resources they have and need to create the changes in their life.

I will say, if you are looking for a simple formula about how to work with people as a Coach, then NLP might not be for you. There are so many different avenues you can take with a person, as you learn the skills of NLP and Coaching you will be able to marry up the different options that will be best for the clients that you work with.

This is actually one of the things that makes NLP Coaching so fun for me — I feel like I'm a puzzle putter-togetherer — I help my clients unpack their outcome with the NLP formula and create the best plan forward for this specific person. I love that!

# CHAPTER 4

# YOU AS A COACH

Often, we are asked what the requirements are to become a Coach – while many Coaches have Bachelor or advanced degrees, many do not. Life experience, passion and desire make up for a lot of formal qualifications.

In our experience, the following characteristics are a sign of someone who will be a great Coach:

- A deep curiosity of humans and human potential
- Flexibility and an agile mindset
- You may already be the 'go to' person for your friends and colleagues
- Motivation/drive to engage and support people

Your life/work experience, and willingness to learn more than what you already know will put you in good stride for becoming a Coach.

Some new Coaches believe that it's the Coaches role to offer advice to their clients; however, this is not the case. The Coach is responsible for empowering their client to find their own answers while helping to encourage, motivate and inspire them to create their own path and achieve their goals.

As such, I wanted to share with you the most common activities that a Coach does:

- A Coach listens
- A Coach supports
- A Coach challenges
- A Coach respects
- A Coach inspires
- A Coach guides
- A Coach is patient
- A Coach strategises
- A Coach collaborates
- A Coach helps
- A Coach asks questions
- A Coach respects

In this chapter we will look at more characteristics and traits that may help you to find out if you will suit Coaching. At the end of the day, if you have the heart and passion to help others, then you are ready to become a Coach.

A Coach doesn't need to be book smart to help other people, you will mainly be using your natural resourcefulness to assist your clients. Through learning specific tools, you will also have the understanding, knowledge and skills to help people identify and clear obstacles in their lives. Nothing could be more enlightening and stimulating than having this privilege in other peoples' lives.

## CHARACTERISTICS OF GREAT COACHES

We've already talked about the demand for Coaches and about the tools you can learn to be a Coach, but one question really remains. Can anyone be a Coach?

The answer is yes…and no.

It's a yes if you're willing to learn how to be a good Coach and apply what you learn through hundreds of hours of sessions with clients.

It's a no if you happen to think that Coaching is just about asking a bunch of questions and hoping your client comes up with the solution himself. It's also a no if you think that Coaching is about telling your client what to do.

The truth is, personal and business Coaching requires a range of skills and attributes.

Here are the top 20 born-to-Coach personality traits you need to know about an aim to possess:

**Compassionate** - Great Coaches are compassionate. They truly feel for their clients and the struggles and challenges they face. They are, first and foremost kind and uplifting. A great Coach never resorts to shaming, threats or scare tactics to motivate a client.

**Supportive** - Great Coaches take their clients' struggles seriously, no matter how small or insignificant these may seem. It doesn't matter if a client is trying to complete a small project or trying to win a battle against cancer; a great Coach is supportive of any and all of these challenges. Great Coaches have an incredible ability to walk a mile in their client's shoes yet retain enough distance to see the big picture and offer guidance and direction.

**Learning Machine** - Great Coaches have an insatiable thirst for knowledge and improvement. They're learning machines. If there's a book, course, program or training that can help them develop themselves, their business or their skills as a Coach, they're on it like ducks to water. A great Coach never gets tired of learning and never ever says "I know enough. I can stop learning now."

**Innovative** - Great Coaches are always looking for ways to level-up their skills and their methodologies. They never get tired of experimenting, switching, upgrading, or changing their Coaching styles and format. In a sea of Coaching experts, innovation sets the great Coach apart from everyone else. Finding and developing a unique or unusual methodology (that works) is key.

**Humble** - Great Coaches are more than happy to learn from their clients. In fact, they're thrilled to learn from them. They're never "know-it- all's" who talk down to clients from the "high horse" of knowledge and power. They're willing to admit mistakes and make things right with a client and they're always willing to learn from other Coaches. No matter how good they become, they're the first to tell you that there's someone better they can learn from.

**Awesome listener** - Great Coaches listen more than they talk. They're not about trying to come across as "clever" or "fascinating" to their clients. They know that client sessions are about the client and not about them. They don't love to hear themselves speak. Often, a truly great Coach gets completely lost in what the client has to say and holds no thought about themselves.

**Curious** - Possibly the most important personality trait of all — a great Coach is curious. They want to know why the client feels a certain way. They want to know what inspires a client, what makes them tick, what puts them off and what keeps them going. They want to know everything there is to know about their clients so they can find the perfect way to help a client.

**Grateful** - Great Coaches are grateful. They're grateful for their clients, their profession and the fact that they're able to help others. This deep gratitude helps them lean into their work and give their best no matter what else is going on in their personal lives. Great Coaches do not take their work or their clients for granted. Ever.

**Excellent communicator** - Great Coaches are able to communicate their message, advice and feedback in a way that really gets through to their clients. They know exactly how to use the right words, language and tone of voice to connect deeply with clients. They also have an incredible ability to adapt to each client individually and say just the right thing in the right way, so it leaves a lasting impression.

**Visionary** - Great Coaches are able to rise above and capture lateral as well as future vision. Lateral vision is about accurately seeing the immediate circumstances around a client's challenge or problem and identifying what needs to be changed. Future vision is about seeing the outcome clients want to achieve and the steps that are needed to get them there.

**Positive** - Great Coaches are positive...to a point. They don't hide the truth just because it's unpleasant. While they're more than happy to inspire a client with a positive, uplifting viewpoint, they're also not afraid to tell it like it is. If a client isn't pulling her weight or making excuses, they'll call her out. Great Coaches know there's a thin line between encouragement and misleading feedback about what's really going on.

**Courageous** - Great Coaches are brave. They're not afraid to try new ways to connect with a client. They're not afraid to set healthy boundaries with clients (like no calling, emailing or messaging nights or weekends), they're not afraid to pull the plug on Coaching sessions if they're dealing with an unresponsive or disinterested client.

**Observant** - Great Coaches are highly observant and have an incredible ability to read between the lines. They're able to pick up and interpret the tiniest change in a client. A shift in the tone of voice, a raised eyebrow, a clearing of the throat and long pauses between sentences. Great Coaches notice all of this and can interpret what they see, hear and feel from a client, accurately.

**Focused** - Great Coaches are focused on their clients throughout a session. They aren't easily distracted and are able to shift into laser focus mode no matter what else is going on. Whether it's a barking dog in the background or a client's child looking for attention from mom or dad, a really great Coach can always bring the conversation back to where it needs to be.

**Dedicated** - A great Coach understands that it takes time to make changes and to see the results of internal and mindset shifts. So, they settle in and make a decision to ride alongside the client through the ups and downs. Even if it takes longer than expected for clients to reach their goals, they will stick around as long as the client is willing to do the work.

**Honest** - A great Coach is honest. They don't lie to their clients just to make them feel better about themselves. If a client needs to know she's not trying hard enough, they'll tell her the truth. If a client needs to know that her goals are too big, they'll tell her that too. Great Coaches are always kind, but they don't shy away from the truth.

**Professional -** A great Coach is never unprofessional. You won't catch them having lunch during a session, turning up looking dishevelled or unkempt or arriving late for a session. They're always punctual and neatly dressed. If necessary, they're ready with notes from previous sessions and they're instantly able to guide a client into the day's discussion.

**Trustworthy -** Great Coaches can be trusted. Period. Clients can be sure that they won't inadvertently come across any of their personal information or challenges revealed, no matter what. Some Coaches discuss their clients' challenges and issues using pseudonyms on social media. A great Coach will never do this. Everything that's discussed during a session stays between the Coach and the client.

**Modelling -** A great Coach believes in modelling. They model others who are more successful or have achieved the goals they want to achieve, and they understand that they need to be a model for their clients too. They follow their own rules and walk their talk. This serves as a wonderful inspiration and reassurance for clients who get to see a Coach's principles, beliefs and teachings play out in real life.

**Sincere -** Great Coaches are heart-centred. They're sincere and they truly care about their clients. They want to help and be of service. They are happy to go above and beyond a client's expectations. Great Coaches don't think of Coaching as a job. It's a calling.

These 20 personality traits will tell you if Coaching is something that will come naturally to you but even if it doesn't, it's nothing to worry about. You can always enhance the attributes you already have and cultivate the ones you don't.

Remember, great Coaches are made not born.

# COACH TRAINING READINESS ASSESSMENT

The following survey comes from Coach U – it provides an exceptional self-assessment to identify if you are ready to pursue Coach training. Simply read the following statements and tick the ones that fit you.

__ I sense things about others that they are surprised about when I share them.

__ I am intuitive and can sense things about people that other people may not.

__ I enjoy helping others solve a problem with which they are struggling.

__ I've got a spark. People comment on how alive I am.

__ I am a very positive person.

__ I am naturally curious about people. I want to learn about them.

__ I am fascinated by life and how it all works.

__ I am excited about the changes in life and I want to stay ahead of the curve.

__ I'm willing to be honest with people, even if its awkward for them or me.

__ I deeply respect people and accept very different ways of thinking.

__ I enjoy being a strategist. I like supporting people in charting their course.

__ I believe people are willing to invest in working with me.

__ I am willing to take the time to learn and perfect the craft of Coaching.

__ I attract people who want my support and input.

__ I am open to learning new concepts and paradigms, even if they don't make sense at first.

__ I can handle paradoxes.

__ I am willing to have my life be a model for others.

__ I am willing to charge for my services (if relevant).

__ I enjoy adding value to whomever I can because I enjoy serving others.

__ I am aware of my limits, yet I know I can Coach others well.

__ I want to learn new Coaching models and technologies to help enhance my skill set and the performance of others.

__ I am willing to learn Coaching skills via ongoing virtual discussions and self-study.

__ I am willing to immerse myself in learning to be a masterful Coach.

__ I care a lot about people and enjoy seeing them achieve their goals.

__ I am excited to help others live their best life.

**If you ticked:**

20-25  You are already a Coach, formal training will enhance your natural strength

15-19  You are an excellent candidate for Coach Training

10-14  Although Coaching may not be the right career for you, learning Coaching skills will certainly improve your current work and quality of life.

0-9  It appears that Coaching would not be a good fit for you, perhaps we could talk about NLP Training for your personal growth

# BECOMING A COACH

Today, it is common to have Coaches who have come from a variety of different occupations. We often see consultants, therapists, trainers, human resource professionals and managers of all types add Coaching skills to their toolbox. It is not uncommon to have lawyers, accountants, business owners and even ministers enter the field of Coaching. Coaching skills benefit everyone who engages with other people, and everyone who wants to achieve better results in their life.

If you already are a Coach, you may be looking at formalizing your Coaching qualifications and becoming a Credentialed Coach with the ICF. If you are just starting out, you probably have questions about how to become a Coach. If you are wanting to start a Coaching practice, you may have questions about getting started with your business. The next two chapters will help answer these questions.

# GET TRAINING

The first step, once you decide that you want to become a Coach is to get adequate training. There are a lot of Coach Trainings available today, in my opinion, you will be looking for an **Accredited Coach Training Program** (ACTP) from the International Coach Federation – you will see this ACTP logo.

The NLP Coach Certification training that I deliver through NLP Worldwide since 2006 is an ACTP course. If you are already a successful Coach, simply wanting to add NLP skills and ICF credentials you may be better suited to our ACSTH (Accredited Coach Specific Train Hours) program offerings which provides less skill refinement than the ACTP and a faster route to accreditation/certification.

The decision to become a Coach and to integrate Coaching skills and competencies into personal and professional life is an important one. If you are seeking a simple qualification without rigorous skill, confidence and competence development, there are trainings available that we can point you towards.

However, if you are seeking exceptional skills, structure, competence and confidence as a Coach, our NLP Coach Certification is one of the best programs available. When we designed this program, it was after my own experience and the combined experiences from many of our students who had completed prior-Coach trainings.

Overall, we found many holes in the different trainings we looked at. Either they were too light on skill development or too heavy on theory.

From a standpoint of integrity, authenticity and quality – our Coach Certification training is not for everyone.

Before, or once our students enrol in the Coach Certification, you will meet with one of our Success Coaches who will conduct your Onboarding – ensuring that you and we know your desires, a timeline for completion and schedule for training. We want to make sure you are set up for success!

The full NLP Coach Certification Training with the Worldwide Institutes of NLP generally takes a total of 6-15 months to complete, based on 5-15 hours per month outside of the in-person trainings. It is a blended learning program comprising of 19 in-person day of group training, online self-paced modules, Coaching practice (either online or in person) and online group supervision.

1.  NLP Level 1: Practitioner Certification (7 days in person + online pre-course)
2.  NLP Level 2: NLP Master Practitioner Certification (9 days in person)
3.  NLP Coaching Foundations (3 days in person or 6 weeks live online)
4.  Coach Building Blocks (self paced)
5.  10 hours of Supervision/Mentoring
6.  Practice

If the training timetable lines up with your schedule and you can dedicate approximately 5 hours per week to your studies, you will see yourself certified as a Coach in about 6 months, and then you can gain the practice you need as a Coach to then gain your credentials with the ICF if you choose.

Let me tell you a little more about each of the aspects of the program and give you an idea of how you might spread the training over 12 months.

## NLP LEVEL 1: PRACTITIONER CERTIFICATION

Your journey to become an NLP Coach begins here. This first level of NLP training will offer you an introduction to the NLP tools, Coaching Core Competencies and self-Coaching themes. While it has a focus on YOU and your personal development, this inevitably leads you to a better understanding of others. This is a 7 day in-person training with online pre-course learning that you will start upon enrolment of the course.

## LEVEL 2: NLP MASTER PRACTITIONER CERTIFICATION

In this program, you will learn to detect patterns, secondary gains and add numerous tools to your toolbox including conversational change, quantum linguistics and advanced techniques to help facilitate growth and personal transformation. This is where the artistry of Coaching really begins. This is a 9 day in-person training. *Pre-requisite: NLP Practitioner Certification*

## NLP COACHING FOUNDATIONS

The focus of this training is to provide you with a structure so you know what to do with your clients, when to do it and why you are doing it. The emphasis is on 4 major core competencies and skill development to ensure you can help lead your client to their successful outcomes. This training is conducted over either 3 days in person, or over 6 weeks online, in-person training. *Pre-requisite: NLP Practitioner Certification*

## NLP COACH BUILDING BLOCKS

Coach Building Blocks is designed to take your Coaching Skills from competent to excellent. The aim of the program is to help you incorporate and improve your NLP skills into a dynamic NLP Coaching practice through 7 robust online training modules. This component is largely self-paced and requires 6-8 months to complete the assignments and assessments.

## COACHING PRACTICE

Continue to gain skills by being involved with our Coaching Graduates to refine, practice and further develop your Coaching skills. We provide ample opportunity for you to Coach (and be Coached) in order to attain the ICF requirement of 100 Coaching hours for Associate Certified Coach credentials.

# EXAMPLE TRAINING PLAN

The following is simply an example training plan spread across 12 months. Your own training plan may differ depending on when the live trainings are scheduled, your availably and your personal momentum. Your Success Coach will help to keep you on track and accountable for completion.

If you wish, before you enrol, **schedule a call with a Success Coach** to ensure the training and course meets your needs and you have the time complete the program.

| Month 1 | Enrol in the program. Start the online pre-course learning – NLP Fundamentals and NLP Communication Essentials |
| --- | --- |
| Month 2 | Continue the pre-course online learning, read **NLP Success Map** |
| Month 3 | Complete the **NLP Practitioner Certification** (7 days) |
| Month 4 | Start the **Coach Building Blocks** online training online, begin peer Coaching |
| Month 5 | Continue with the Coach Building Blocks and peer Coaching, Start the online **Build your Business Workshop** and begin group supervision. |

| Month 6 | Complete the **NLP Master Practitioner** (9 days) OR **NLP Coaching Foundations** (3 days or 6 weeks live online) and continue with Coach Building Blocks. |
|---|---|
| Month 7 | Continue with Coach Building Blocks and peer Coaching & group supervision and start working with paid clients |
| Month 8 | Continue with Coach Building Blocks and peer Coaching & group supervision and start working with paid clients |
| Month 9 | Complete the NLP Master Practitioner OR NLP Coaching Foundations and continue with Coach Building Blocks. |
| Month 10 | Continue with Coach Building Blocks and peer Coaching & group supervision and start working with paid clients |
| Month 11 | Continue with Coach Building Blocks, continue with peer Coaching, supervision and working with paid clients. |
| Month 12 | Complete the Coach Building Blocks, continue with peer Coaching, supervision and working with paid clients. |

Once you have completed all training and supervision, you will be awarded with Certification as an NLP Certified Coach. You can apply to the ICF once you have logged 100 Coaching hours.

## ONGOING LEARNING

We recommend you continue your learning – if you join the ICF, there is an ongoing learning requirement of 40 hours of Continuing Coach Education (CCE) to be completed every 3 years. To be included in NLP Worldwide's online Coach list we require 20 hours of ongoing learning per year. One of the best ways to obtain this ongoing learning is to continue to advanced levels of training – or, sometimes an even better (and more cost-effective option), is to review the NLP trainings a second (or third) time as a student again.

We offer all of our students the ability to review any of their previous trained levels of NLP or Coaching – often for free or for a minimal cost. Think of this as watching your favourite movie for a third or fourth time – you always learn something new; and it's always great to get back to the basics!  Experienced Coaches tend to lean on their favourite tools, and it is very beneficial to review your earlier learning.

## GET PRACTICE

You start practicing Coaching from the day you enrol in the NLP Coach Certification and login to the Student Membership site to get started on the pre-course learning. You will start with the NLP Fundamentals and Communication Essentials online trainings – which will provide you with tools and skills to  use in every interpersonal interaction from that moment onward.

When you step into the training room for your first official day of Coach training, you are walking into a Coaching System. During the training you will be trying on various skills as both the *Coach* and *Client*. During and after your certification trainings, we encourage you to get involved in our in-person and online practice groups, Coach Mentoring program and Coaching triads when they come up.

You will truly learn to Coach well by Coaching others within the first few months of starting your training. We suggest starting to work with your fellow students right away, and our Graduates network is globally massive. As soon as your confidence has grown, it is advisable you start working with clients too. Tell your family, friends and co-workers what you are doing and perhaps they have friends who would like to work with you as their Coach!

With time, experience and feedback, you will become a highly masterful Coach. We know you will never become *masterful* without practice, so it's better to dive right in! We've seen that our students who are actively involved in Coaching tend to get more out of their Coach training.

# SUPERVISION & MENTORING

If I could give my younger self who was becoming a Coach any gift at all, I would give her a Supervisor!  Clinical Supervision & Mentoring is not a requirement of most Coach training programs, but it is in ours – and it is for the ICF and a few NLP Associations. I absolutely love Supervision, both as the Supervisee and Supervisor.

Each month, I run a few online group supervision programs where a small group of Coaches get together to share our wins and challenges, confidentially discuss client scenarios and help each other out.

I also run a Coach Mentoring group a few times each year where 5 Coaches come together for 6 weeks and Coach each other and receive feedback on their Coaching skills, give each other feedback and learn from each other. I also benchmark the Coaching skills using a best-practice benchmark to give feedback about what the Coach is doing well and what they can improve upon. This proves extremely beneficial while developing skills as a Coach. If possible, I would make this a mandatory program annually for all Coaches in their first 4 years of Coaching.

Additionally, Supervision is beneficial to watch for transference and counter transference – that is, the Coach either taking on their clients' issues or projecting their life onto the client. Having someone, or a group, be accountable regarding self-care is an important aspect of Coaching. As a Coach, you are only as effective for your clients as you are for yourself.

From time to time, you may request a Coaching Audit from your Supervisor – this entails providing a video or audio recording of a client session to be evaluated for feedback. In our Coach Certification training we use a Benchmarking model which specifies the ICF-determined Coaching skills best practices– your Supervisor can assist you to ensure your skills are growing and you are developing your competence as an exceptional Coach.

A Coach that is learning, is a Coach that is growing – and they often have the best success for their clients.

# GETTING COACHED

You encourage your clients to have a Coach, it only seems right to have one yourself doesn't it?

Not only do we encourage our students to start Coaching others, practice their skills deliberately and participate in Supervision; we also know the value of *being Coached.* If you join us for our NLP Coach Certification, the program includes six one-on-one personal Coaching sessions with one of our Senior Coaches. Having your own Coach is beneficial for three reasons:

1. You get to experience Coaching like your clients do, so you have a better understanding of the process
2. You are able to continue to work on 'your stuff', helping you to be the best person and Coach you can be
3. You learn more about various Coaching styles and can work on any topic at all with your Coach – including your business!

Most of our Coaches continue to work with a personal Coach as an ongoing personal evolvement tool well past their Certification is complete.

# CHAPTER 5

# THE BUSINESS OF COACHING

If you choose to become a Coach with a private practice, there will be tasks of setting up your business. This isn't applicable to all Coaches. You may want to use your Coaching skills in your current (or new) job, you may work for someone else, you might want to volunteer your Coaching skills, or you may simply want to be a hobbyist Coach.

This chapter will be relevant if you are someday looking to build a business of your own. Some basic business and entrepreneurial skills will be very useful to do this – the business of Coaching isn't always an easy one, it takes work and dedication to get the business off the ground, much like any other business.

Like in all other sections of this book, I'm going to be honest. There are so many Coach trainings available that will make promises of big incomes, part time hours with fulltime pay and travelling the world while Coaching when you can fit it in. I have no doubt that there are some Coaches that have achieved those things. I also know that most people who want to be Coaches and who make it as a Coach, want to help others, not live in a get-rich-quick model.

You know the saying *if it's too good to be true it probably is*, I think that applies to a lot of the shiny marketing ploys to get you to train with them. I have experienced and have learned what it takes to make a

Coaching business successful and I'm going to share as much as I can of this with you now. For the rest, you can join me at NLP Worldwide. I think the more you know before you embark upon becoming a Coach the better! I tell you none of this to scare you off, but rather to prepare you for the journey ahead.

Learning the business development side of business is important – it ultimately may be what sets people up for success or failure. Big dreams but little planning and action is a sure-fire way to be a Coach for only a short amount of time.

The business development side of Coaching is about reaching the right people, being relevant for those people and creating revenue. Even if you complete the best training in the world and develop the best Coaching skills in the world, if no one knows about you and if you are not creating a sustainable income, you can't make your business flourish, grow and last. Sustainable income equals a maintainable business.

Here are the main steps for creating and setting up your business. Some of this can be done now, before you complete your Coach training, and some of it would be best done after:

# STEP 1: DECIDE WHO YOU WANT TO COACH

In today's world of internet marketing, key word searching and website optimisation, especially in the beginning creates clarity of explanation and advertising of your business. As you gain experience and clients, it's easier to diversify, but in the early days it is wise to choose one to three areas of specialisation.

When you start this selection process, start thinking about what types of people and problems do you encounter regularly? If you are already in contact with your target market, this will make it easier to reach them. For example, are you a parent, or manager? Do you have sales experience or perhaps knowledge of relationship breakdowns? All of this can help you begin to figure out who you want to work with.

Begin to think about the type of people you want to help (parents, women, people in transition), and the types of problems they might experience. It may also be useful to brainstorm what is important to you about this type of person/problem to help identify other possible target clients.

While I don't necessarily believe that you need to have experienced what you Coach, identifying what you have overcome in your life is a beneficial exercise to think about. These potential clients may be the simplest to attract, which is the main aim for the first few years of your business while you gain more confidence, credibility and skill.

# STEP 2: CREATE A SERVICE THAT PEOPLE WILL PAY FOR

Let's be honest. There are a lot of Coaches out there. I mean, a lot! But there is only one you.

For you to be successful as a Coach, not only do you need to figure out who you want to help and what you want to help them with, you need to create a service that is (a) easy to explain and understand and (b) something that people want to pay for.

So – find the problems people have that you can solve. And, as I've mentioned, in the beginning, find one, two or three problems. The more skilled and known you get the easier it will be to diversify. But, stating early in your Coaching, "I can help you create the life you want", might be just a tad too big.

Let's even start here – do you want to work with people in an ad-hoc manner, working hour-to-hour with your clients? Or, do you want to create packages?

Packages can be structured or unstructured – and most Coach-marketing gurus will tell you this is the way to go.

I say, do whatever works for you and your clients. I've never had packages, I've always only worked hour-to-hour with my clients, and it works for me. But it may not work for you.

When I first started, I was working with people on average between 8-12 one-hour appointments. As my skills improved, I now work with most people between 4-6 one-hour appointments.

However, you can choose whether to work with people in a packaged way. Structured packages are a great idea for new Coaches who want to have something tangible to offer to their clients with a specified outcome. Here are two examples of 4 session packages. Each of the elements I mention in the packages are based on NLP tools you will learn in the training. Please note, you can create any number of packages for as few or as many sessions as you desire:

| | LIFE BALANCE COACHING | CONFIDENCE COACHING |
|---|---|---|
| WEEK 1 | Elicit values on 2 areas of life | Client Intake Questions |
| WEEK 2 | Identify interferences and clear these | Build resources and create a confidence anchor |
| WEEK 3 | Access and build resources | Align confidence with values and meta programs |
| WEEK 4 | Create personal alignment and add a goal in the future | Identify and clear interferences, enhance state of confidence |

Generally, with any type of package, you contract your clients for a certain amount of time or outcome, and charge your client (usually up front, sometimes on a short payment plan) for the full program. You will need to investigate having strong Terms and Conditions for packages.

If you choose to have an unstructured package – this simply means that you are doing more *ad-hoc* Coaching but charging for a certain number of sessions.

In the NLP Coach Certification training, you will learn a strategy to use with your clients that will allow you to know what to do in each session, how to do it and more importantly, why you are doing it. So, those unstructured sessions do become somewhat structured, but based on what the client brings to you as their present and desired state (remember the NLP Formula?).

Another idea to think about is to have tasks between sessions. You can create guided audio programs, webinars, e-books, online lessons,, tools or exercises that will keep your client involved. You may also choose to have an email exchange or a quick 15-minute phone or Zoom catchup between sessions (depending on how long between sessions), or you may provide accountability Coaching between sessions.

Whatever you do, keep it simple. It must be easy to explain and understand. And you don't have to decide on anything now. This is just food for thought before you complete your training.

## STEP 3: DECIDE ON YOUR PRICING

It is common for professional Coaches to be charging hundreds of dollars per hour across the globe. While we cannot promise you will receive any financial compensation for your services, we know many of our students seem to be generating $80,000-$150,000 per year. We can confidently say that experienced, highly competent, confident, focused, hardworking and business-minded Coaches can earn a nice living doing meaningful work.

Most of our Coaching students start Coaching within four to six months of entering the training program. Sometimes charging, sometimes for free while learning. Over the past two decades, we've learned that some of the best Coaches get started Coaching as soon as they feel capable and their competence and confidence grows from there. When people wait to feel confident and competent before starting to Coach, they sometimes never start Coaching!

To choose your price point, you need to do some research about how much other Coaches change with similar skills, qualifications and experience in your vicinity. Hourly rates and packages may have different price points depending on the time and services offered.

It is fair to say that as you gain experience you can ethically raise your fees, but in the beginning being more modest will be more integral. This will go against any marketing guru or cowboy trainer, they will tell you to start charging top dollar out of the gate; if you are comfortable and congruent with that, by all means, go for it!

One suggestion I often offer to my students is to choose a fairly modest price point (for example $50 per hour if you are not yet certified, $80 if you are certified, $100 if you are ACC credentialed with the ICF), and for every 50 Coaching hours you do, raise your fee by $20 per hour until you are at the rate you finally desire. This strategy allows you to get paid from the moment you start and helps you to increase your rate as your skills improve.

For me, this was important. When I first started out, I stumbled a lot and took nearly double the amount of time with clients than I do now. For example, when I was learning I would work with someone for 12 sessions, whereas I now work with that same person for only 4-6 sessions. The more experience you get, the better you will become and the less time you will tend to work with a client on one issue.

If in doubt of when to start Coaching, simply stay in close contact with us and we will let you know when your skill-base is solid enough to start applying your NLP Coaching skills with others.

# STEP 4: CREATE A MARKETING STRATEGY

A lot a new Coach's time should go into marketing. In fact, the whole administrative side of the business (marketing, banking, accounts, creating programs and products, etc.) takes up a great deal of time. The fun part of Coaching is the Coaching. But the marketing strategy can be fun too.

These days, a lot of people outsource the marketing of their Coaching business to other people. They engage a copywriter to write blog posts, a social media manager to post on social media and even someone to create and send emails to prospective clients. While this may sound all well and good, I am yet to see it work long term. Either the Coach runs out of money, or they realise the money they are spending is not getting much return on investment.

From what I have seen, marketing is very personal. If you are simply getting pretty memes with motivational quotes made and posted on social media – you may get some *likes* (if people see them), but do those images actually fit for what and who you are marketing too?

I have personally tried outsourcing some of the marketing efforts for NLP Worldwide and I regretted it. I spent money unwisely, losing time and possible contacts because the voice they were using was not my own. I learned that most outsourced marketing agencies hire people with no prior experience to create and post images – and at the end of the day, the marketing agencies don't know your business better than you do.

I would highly recommend finding some relatively inexpensive online marketing workshops to teach yourself optimal marketing. Udemy has a lot of great training on it – and, a lot of not so great ones too, but enough to help you learn what you need to know.

Social Media (like Facebook, Instagram, Twitter and Linked In) are great passive marketing avenues. Because people are not actively searching for a Coach, they will see your posts or advertisements because of targeting. However, you are always dependent upon catching readers at a good time - do they want to read what you are sharing, be in the mood to click, pay attention and take action.

Unless you know that social media is going to be a phenomenal place to attract clients, spend money on Search Engine Optimisation and things like Google AdWords instead of investing in social media; you know that people seeing you through searches are actively looking for Coaches.

That doesn't mean don't use social media – by all means do! Social media will give you what is known as *social proof* and have a way to attract possible clients to share their details with you. This is known as a *lead magnet*. Lead magnets are things like videos, webinar, downloadables, surveys, etc., basically you are trading something of value for the contact details of the prospective client.

You'll need to invest in some sort of back end software (could be a website plugin, Mail Chimp, A-Webber, Infusionsoft, etc.) that will collect the contact details from your web funnels and offer you the ability to follow up by email or text.

As you generate income, you may want to invest in something more substantial that will allow you to create autoresponders (emails that are sent automatically in a sequence) that will help you to continue to reach out and nurture your prospective clients.

A recent study showed that Coaching clients required on average of 6-8 touch points from a passive lead (e.g. From Facebook), before they will engage in services. This means that you will need to have a marketing stream or way to nurture those people in your potential client funnel.

Creating give away products like an e-book, a webinar, a pre-recorded e-learning, an audio recording or podcast, a survey or whitepaper will be very beneficial. Make a few things that resonate with you and for your clients. Whatever you use as your lead magnets need to be authentic and aligned to you as a Coach. There are sites that you can purchase this collateral from, but make sure if you do this, it is still united with your message and vision.

Having a website, landing page or Coach Directory listing will be imperative for people to find you and learn more about you. This could be your LinkedIn or Facebook page, but it probably isn't. One thing about that – buy a domain name (you can pick one up pretty cheap) and get an email address to match. There isn't much less professional than a lovely domain name for a website and @gmail.com for email. Let it all match!

I would recommend not spending too much in the beginning – you can create or setup a website for very low cost. Once you are making some money, you can put some back into improvements and scaling of your marketing materials.

Remember blogs, vlogs, YouTube channels, guest posting and sharing on other channels to reach more people in your target audience.

For the first two years of your business, make it your mission to get your name and reputation known. Ask for referrals, create networks to cross promote and share yourself and your services everywhere you can.

I've seen too many wantrapreneures try to be Coaches and their marketing efforts are a few Facebook posts and lots of dollars going into social media marketing.

Remember – social media is for social proof. It helps you to get seen, but don't get swept up into making it a sales channel. If you have amazing products that will go viral, then we're talking a different story (and business!). For marketing, really get clear about who you want to work with and how to reach them, educate them about what you do, and have them choose you!

# STEP 5: DECIDE WHEN AND WHERE YOU WILL COACH & WORK

Most Coaches love what they do because they enjoy assisting people to achieve what they want most in life. Not just that, you can have flexibility of when and where you work from.

Many Coaches have created 100% online Coaching practice working from Skype, Zoom or the phone – this allows you the opportunity to work from anywhere in the world. You can also work from an office, create a cohort of Coaches to go in on renting an office together, use co-working spaces or even seek permission to work regularly from the office of a business client you have.

You also have the option of setting your hours – will you be providing Coaching during working hours, evenings or on the weekend?

Especially in the beginning, when you are just starting out, there is not a need to spend much money at all. Some of our Coach students meet their clients at the local library where they use a sound-proof room, others meet at a coffee shop or in the park. We even have one student who does *Walking Coaching* where he will meet his client somewhere in the city and walk and talk.

You can choose to even work from home – either part time, or full time). If working from home, it is recommended that you have a separate space for your business work away from home distractions. Your options are endless.

We also recommend defining work hours and sticking to them, regardless if you have clients or not.

For example, you may choose to start your Coaching business part time on Monday and Tuesday from 9am to 5pm. When you dedicate yourself to this time ritually – to work on your business AND to work with clients, you are creating healthy habits and setting yourself up for success by committing to a structure for your business.

We have seen many new Coaches have an attitude of "I don't have clients today, so I have the day off" – a lot of your time in the first many months, if not many years, will be spent working ON the business – marketing, advertising, strategizing, planning, organising, filing and creating. Although this isn't usually the part of the business that makes a Coach's heart sing, it is a very important part of the business.

As a rule of thumb, for the first few years of developing your Coaching practice (if you want to create a full-time income), estimate 3 hours of administrative work (marketing, planning, preparing for clients, accounts, etc.) for 1 hour of client work. This means that if you intend to work with 10 clients per week, you have a 40 hour per week job.

Over time this will decrease as you get more referrals, streamline your marketing and solidify your lead magnets – but the work on the business will always be there. You might as well set up your workspace and work hours to match success.

## STEP 6: DECIDE IF YOU WILL ADD OTHER SERVICES

While you learn the skills of Coaching, you will also be gaining more understanding where these skills can also be used to take you and your clients to the next level; perhaps even elevating yourself to the next level.

Many Coaches develop training or group Coaching events, write books, conduct webinars, publish newsletters, conduct research, provide workshops, conduct speaking engagements and more.

It isn't uncommon for Coaches to take their skills into groups, communities and teams to provide additional services including consulting and training. In fact, many of our NLP Coaching students continue on with our NLP Trainer & Consultant Certification, which unpacks the NLP tools for using NLP from one-to-many.

# CHAPTER 6

# THE INTERNATIONAL COACH FEDERATION

The International Coach Federation (ICF), is the largest worldwide, non-profit, professional association for personal and business Coaches.

The ICF exists to build, support and preserve the integrity of the Coaching profession around the globe by creating, maintaining and upgrading the standards of the profession.

Here at NLP Worldwide, we recognise the importance of credentialing with the ICF and we support and facilitate the process by providing Accredited Coach Training Programs (ACTP).

The ICF Credentialing Program exists to:

1. Protect consumers of Coaching services (and serve as an indicator of quality, assurance that someone can provide the services they are credentialed to provide.
2. Measure competence (presently done with a combination of knowledge test and a performance test).
3. Inspire growth of the individual.

The ICF credential is awarded to professional Coaches and Coach training programs that meet or exceed the minimum standards.

# GETTING CREDENTIALED WITH THE ICF

While you do not have to pursue credentialing with the ICF, it is highly recommended. The ICF has done an amazing job of educating the public about Coaching and the standards they have set. If you are looking to do more Business or Executive Coaching, it is nearly a necessity these days to have your ICF credentials. If you work in Human Resources or Leadership – ICF credentials are one of the most sought-after credentials today.

For life, wellness and transition Coaches, this credential is not imperative, but the added level of credibility the ICF gives is very beneficial for your brand and promotion, especially for new Coaches.

There are three pathways to becoming credentialed with the ICF, we can help with all of them. The NLP Coach Certification program with NLP Worldwide is an Accredited Coach Training Program (ACTP) with the ICF, meaning all of the ACTP training and assessment criteria is included in our Coach Certification training. If you are new to Coaching, I recommend the ACTP pathway which will provide you with everything you need. If you are more of an experienced Coach, the ACSTH pathway may suffice.

## ACTP PATHWAY

**Requirements:**

- Completion of an entire ICF Accredited Coach Training Program (ACTP). (the NLP Worldwide Coach Certification course is an ACTP training)

- A minimum of 100 hours (75 paid) of Coaching experience with at least eight clients following the start of your Coach-specific training. At least 25 of these hours must occur within the 18 months prior to submitting the application for the credential.

- Completion of the Coach Knowledge Assessment (CKA)

**Pricing & Timeframe:**
- $300 USD
- Estimated 4 weeks to review

# ACSTH PATHWAY

**Requirements:**
- At least 60 hours of Coach-specific training through an ACTP or ACSTH program. (the NLP Worldwide Coach Training meets this)

- 10 hours of Mentor Coaching over a minimum of three months to be documented on your online application. Your Mentor Coach must be an ACC who has completed a full cycle of the credential through renewal, PCC or MCC in good standing.
- A minimum of 100 hours (75 paid) of Coaching experience with at least eight clients following the start of your Coach-specific training. At least 25 of these hours must occur within the 18 months prior to submitting the application for the credential.
- Performance evaluation (audio recording and written transcript of a Coach session to be uploaded with your application).
- Completion of the Coach Knowledge Assessment (CKA).

**Pricing & Timeframe:**
- $500 USD
- Estimated 14 weeks to review

For more information on the various pathways for becoming a credentialed member of the ICF please visit:

https://Coachfederation.org/icf-credential/acc-paths

# ICF CORE COMPETENCIES

The following eleven core Coaching competencies were developed to support greater understanding about the skills and approaches used within today's Coaching profession as defined by the International Coach Federation. They will also support you in calibrating the level of alignment between the Coach-specific training expected and the training you have experienced.

Finally, these competencies and the ICF definition were used as the foundation for the ICF Coach Knowledge Assessment (CKA). The ICF defines Coaching as partnering with clients in a thought-provoking and creative process that inspires them to maximize their personal and professional potential. The Core Competencies are grouped into four clusters according to those that fit together logically based on common ways of looking at the competencies in each group. The groupings and individual competencies are not weighted—they do not represent any kind of priority in that they are all core or critical for any competent Coach to demonstrate.

**A. Setting the Foundation**
1. Meeting Ethical Guidelines and Professional Standards
2. Establishing the Coaching Agreement

**B. Co-creating the Relationship**
3. Establishing Trust and Intimacy with the Client
4. Coaching Presence

**C. Communicating Effectively**
5. Active Listening
6. Powerful Questioning
7. Direct Communication

**D. Facilitating Learning and Results**
8. Creating Awareness
9. Designing Actions

10. Planning and Goal Setting
11. Managing Progress and Accountability

See the ICF website for more detailed description:
https://Coachfederation.org/core-competencies

# ICF CODE OF ETHICS

ICF is committed to maintaining and promoting excellence in Coaching. Therefore, ICF expects all members and credentialed Coaches (Coaches, Coach mentors, Coaching supervisors, Coach trainers or students), to adhere to the elements and principles of ethical conduct: to be competent and integrate ICF Core Competencies effectively in their work.

In line with the ICF core values and ICF definition of Coaching, the Code of Ethics is designed to provide appropriate guidelines, accountability and enforceable standards of conduct for all ICF Members and ICF Credential-holders, who commit to abiding by the following ICF Code of Ethics:

## Part One: Definitions

- Coaching: Coaching is partnering with clients in a thought-provoking and creative process that inspires them to maximize their personal and professional potential.

- ICF Coach: An ICF Coach agrees to practice the ICF Core Competencies and pledges accountability to the ICF Code of Ethics.

- Professional Coaching Relationship: A professional Coaching relationship exists when Coaching includes an agreement (including contracts) that defines the responsibilities of each party.

- Roles in the Coaching Relationship: In order to clarify roles in the Coaching relationship it is often necessary to distinguish between the client and the sponsor. In most cases, the client and sponsor are the same person and are therefore jointly referred to as the client. For purposes of identification, however, the ICF defines these roles as follows:

- Client: The "Client/Coachee" is the person(s) being Coached.

- Sponsor: The "sponsor" is the entity (including its representatives) paying for and/or arranging for Coaching services to be provided. In all cases, Coaching engagement agreements should clearly establish the rights, roles and responsibilities for both the client and sponsor if the client and sponsor are different people.

- Student: The "student" is someone enrolled in a Coach training program or working with a Coaching supervisor or Coach mentor in order to learn the Coaching process or enhance and develop their Coaching skills.

- Conflict of Interest: A situation in which a Coach has a private or personal interest sufficient to appear to influence the objective of his or her official duties as a Coach and a professional.

## Part Two: The ICF Standards of Ethical Conduct
## Section 1: Professional Conduct at Large

As a Coach, I:

1) conduct myself in accordance with the ICF Code of Ethics in all interactions, including Coach training, Coach mentoring and Coach supervisory activities.

2) commit to take the appropriate action with the Coach, trainer, or Coach mentor and/or will contact ICF to address any ethics violation or possible breach as soon as I become aware, whether it involves me or others.

3) communicate and create awareness in others, including organizations, employees, sponsors, Coaches and others, who might need to be informed of the responsibilities established by this Code.

4) refrain from unlawful discrimination in occupational activities, including age, race, gender orientation, ethnicity, sexual orientation, religion, national origin or disability.

5) make verbal and written statements that are true and accurate about what I offer as a Coach, the Coaching profession or ICF.

6) accurately identify my Coaching qualifications, expertise, experience, training, certifications and ICF Credentials.

7) recognize and honour the efforts and contributions of others and only claim ownership of my own material. I understand that violating this standard may leave me subject to legal remedy by a third party.

8) strive at all times to recognize my personal issues that may impair, conflict with or interfere with my Coaching performance or my professional Coaching relationships. I will promptly seek the relevant professional assistance and determine the action to be taken, including whether it is appropriate to suspend or terminate my Coaching relationship(s) whenever the facts and circumstances necessitate.

9) recognize that the Code of Ethics applies to my relationship with Coaching clients, Coachees, students, mentees and supervisees.

10) conduct and report research with competence, honesty and within recognized scientific standards and applicable subject guidelines. My research will be carried out with the necessary consent and approval of those involved, and with an approach that will protect participants from any potential harm. All research efforts will be performed in a manner that complies with all the applicable laws of the country in which the research is conducted.

11) maintain, store and dispose of any records, including electronic files and communications, created during my Coaching engagements in a manner that promotes confidentiality, security and privacy and complies with any applicable laws and agreements.

12) use ICF Member contact information (email addresses, telephone numbers, and so on) only in the manner and to the extent authorized by the ICF.

## Section 2: Conflicts of Interest

As a Coach, I:

13) seek to be conscious of any conflict or potential conflict of interest, openly disclose any such conflict and offer to remove myself when a conflict arises.

14) clarify roles for internal Coaches, set boundaries and review with stakeholders' conflicts of interest that may emerge between Coaching and other role functions.

15) Disclose to my client and the sponsor(s) all anticipated compensation from third parties that I may receive for referrals of clients or pay to receive clients.

16) Honour an equitable Coach/client relationship, regardless of the form of compensation.

## Section 3: Professional Conduct with Clients

As a Coach, I:

17) Ethically speak what I know to be true to clients, prospective clients or sponsors about the potential value of the Coaching process or of me as a Coach.

18) Carefully explain and strive to ensure that, prior to or at the initial meeting, my Coaching client and sponsor(s) understand the nature of Coaching, the nature and limits of confidentiality, financial arrangements, and any other terms of the Coaching agreement.

19) Have a clear Coaching service agreement with my clients and sponsor(s) before beginning the Coaching relationship and honour this agreement. The agreement shall include the roles, responsibilities and rights of all parties involved.

20) Hold responsibility for being aware of and setting clear, appropriate and culturally sensitive boundaries that govern interactions, physical or otherwise, I may have with my clients or sponsor(s).

21) Avoid any sexual or romantic relationship with current clients or sponsor(s) or students, mentees or supervisees. Further, I will be alert to the possibility of any potential sexual intimacy among the parties including my support staff and/or assistants and will take the appropriate action to address the issue or cancel the engagement in order to provide a safe environment overall.

22) Respect the client's right to terminate the Coaching relationship at any point during the process, subject to the provisions of the agreement. I shall remain alert to indications that there is a shift in the value received from the Coaching relationship.

23) Encourage the client or sponsor to make a change if I believe the client or sponsor would be better served by another Coach or by another resource and suggest my client seek the services of other professionals when deemed necessary or appropriate.

## Section 4: Confidentiality/Privacy

As a Coach, I:

24) Maintain the strictest levels of confidentiality with all client and sponsor information unless release is required by law.

25) Have a clear agreement about how Coaching information will be exchanged among Coach, client and sponsor.

26) Have a clear agreement when acting as a Coach, Coach mentor, Coaching supervisor or trainer, with both client and sponsor, student, mentee, or supervisee about the conditions under which confidentiality may not be maintained (e.g., illegal activity, pursuant to valid court order or subpoena; imminent or likely risk of danger to self or to others; etc) and make sure both client and sponsor, student, mentee, or supervisee voluntarily and knowingly agree in writing to that limit of

confidentiality. Where I reasonably believe that because one of the above circumstances is applicable, I may need to inform appropriate authorities.

27) Require all those who work with me in support of my clients to adhere to the ICF Code of Ethics, Number 26, Section 4, Confidentiality and Privacy Standards, and any other sections of the Code of Ethics that might be applicable.

## Section 5: Continuing Development

As a Coach, I:

28) Commit to the need for continued and ongoing development of my professional skills.

## Part Three: The ICF Pledge of Ethics

As an ICF Coach, I acknowledge and agree to honour my ethical and legal obligations to my Coaching clients and sponsors, colleagues, and to the public at large. I pledge to comply with the ICF Code of Ethics and to practice these standards with those whom I Coach, teach, mentor or supervise.

If I breach this Pledge of Ethics or any part of the ICF Code of Ethics, I agree that the ICF in its sole discretion may hold me accountable for so doing. I further agree that my accountability to the ICF for any breach may include sanctions, such as loss of my ICF Membership and/or my ICF Credentials.

# CHAPTER 7

# FREQUENTLY ASKED QUESTIONS

### CAN I EARN A LIVING AS A COACH?

Yes, you can. Generally, it takes about six months for people to start generating an income and up to about four years to create a full-time Coaching practice. The more people you know and the smarter you work, the faster you can build your business. We offer resources on starting your business, gaining clients and getting plenty of practice to develop your skills. How successful your business is, depends greatly on your marketing efforts, your level of competence and confidence as well the size and strength of your market. The fun and rewarding part of Coaching is working with clients, but the work behind the scenes to get the clients in the first place is where your focus needs to be for the first few years.

We've found that after a couple years, many Coaches are earning between $50,000-$100,000, and some earn much more than this.

### WHAT DO COACHES DO OTHER THAN COACH INDIVIDUALS?

In additional to Coaching, Coaches often offer other services that balance or complement their Coaching. This may include group or team Coaching, conducting workshops and seminars, offering webinars and other online trainings, conducting presentations, writing books and consulting.

For me, my trifecta of services includes Coaching, Training and Consulting. Often I will be engaged by an organisation, company or group to do a needs analysis for one piece of work (Coaching, for example). From the needs analysis I might identify that a group of people need training in a new mindset or skill or they could benefit from consulting within various teams or perhaps leadership could benefit from individual Coaching. This combination of services is a winning blend, specifically when working with teams, companies and organisations.

For this extra level of training, be sure to ask us about our NLP Trainer & Consultant Certification.

## WHAT LICENSING IS REQUIRED TO BE A COACH?

Currently, there are virtually no governmental licensing requirements for Coaching. The field at this time is very self-regulated, with organisations like the International Coach Federation (ICF), leading the charge for standards, ethics and core competencies. It is now becoming more and more important to become an ICF Certified Coach since clients and companies are being more educated and are more likely than ever to ask you for your credentials.

## CAN A PERSON BE A PART-TIME COACH?

In the beginning at least, most Coaches do work part-time. If you already have a job or business, it would be useful to set aside a few evenings and perhaps a Saturday morning to start your Coaching business. As you work with more clients you will develop more confidence and competence as a Coach – and you may want to transition to full-time Coaching. Of course, you can continue to work as a part-time Coach forever if you choose to!

## How long would a client work with a Coach?

With NLP Coaching, you have an option to work in an adhoc manner or on a project basis with your clients. Generally, you will be working with a client for between 4-8 individual sessions or for between 3-12 months on a project basis, for one Coaching topic. For me, many of my clients roll from topic to topic — so often, I'm working with the same client for many years.

As you become more skilled as a Coach, you'll notice your clients will stay with you longer, working on different topics. They will continue to achieve better results because you are helping them to expand their capacity for growth.

## When should I start working with clients?

As soon as you have gained some basic skills of listening, questioning and identifying the elements of a powerful Coaching conversation, you can start Coaching. The more you Coach — even for free — the more you will benefit from your training.

We have programs in place that you can participate in after your NLP Practitioner training to work with fellow-students, and many people start practicing a few weeks after their initial training. Some people wait until they have gained a few more skills from the NLP Master Practitioner or Coaching Foundations training.

Ultimately, it is entirely up to you — we will also help direct you based on the skills and confidence we see you display in the training room.

## WHAT DOES IT COST TO BECOME A COACH?

From our research, training to become a Coach costs anywhere from $500 for a cheap online training to over $50,000 for a university degree. For ICF accredited training, the cost is between $8,000-$15000 and takes between 6 months to 3 years to complete the training.

Our NLP Coach Certification training costs just under $10,000 – this is for the full ICF accredited Coach training plus a variety of *extras*. We want to set you up for success as a Coach by providing you with the tools, skills, feedback and experience it will take for you to become an exceptional Coach.

I think it's important to note that our course is not necessarily an *easy* one. There are quicker and probably cheaper ways to become a Coach. But our focus is on assisting our students to develop quality Coaching skills that will help them to help others.

## HOW LONG DOES IT TAKE TO BECOME A COACH?

The training required for the NLP Coach Certification will take between 6-18, depending on your timing and motivation. Generally, we find that most people complete the course in 6-9 months, based on about 5 hours per week.

If you choose to start Coaching *during* your training, then you will become a Coach in much less time than if you start Coaching *after* you complete your training. What we've found is that when a person starts Coaching while they are learning, this increases their confidence and competence with the Coaching skills. However, when people wait until they have all the training, they often also wait for the confidence to come too. However, with Coaching, confidence doesn't come before practice, it comes because of practice.

## DO YOU HELP ME GET CLIENTS OR START MY BUSINESS?

If you join us for the NLP Coach Certification, we will equip you with resources, skills and Coaching to start your business – but starting it and getting clients is up to you.

We will provide you with a Coach Business Plan template, online learning about marketing and growing your business and support in the way of Coaching and answering your questions. Once you have completed the training, you will be able to have a listing on our website, which may help drive traffic to you, but this is still in the domain of your responsibility.

## HOW DO I START?

If you are ready to start – please schedule a call with one of our Success Coaches. We will be able to answer any questions you have, create a plan and make sure our Coach Training meets your needs *and* that you are committed to the time and resources needed to complete the program. We allow a maximum of 20 participants in any of our trainings at one time, so be sure to schedule your call soon.

Once you are enrolled, we'll then connect you with a Transformation Team Member for your Coach Onboarding where we'll get you setup with your login to the Student Membership site and get you started with the pre-course learning tools which includes:
- ✓ e-copy of our 30 Days to NLP Book
- ✓ NLP Success Map
- ✓ NLP Fundamentals video series
- ✓ NLP Communications video series

# CHAPTER 8

# WHERE TO FROM HERE?

I hope this book has helped you to know more about becoming a Coach. I truly hope it has inspired you to know that you've got what it takes to be a Coach. We have a phenomenal Coach Training Program and since 1994 we have been helping people to help people.

The first step from here is to get in touch with us and schedule a call with one of our NLP Success Coaches. We will call you (just tell us your number and choose a day and time that works for you), and we will answer any of your questions and ask you some of our own. Ultimately, we want you to know that this course fits what you are looking for and we want to ensure that you have the desire and time to complete the program. We offer payment plans if needed to help spread the costs across many months – be sure to talk to your Success Coach about this option.



We offer the NLP Coach Certification in Sydney, Australia; Singapore and Denver, Colorado, USA. There is a possibility that you may need to travel to where we are conducting the trainig so you can train with our program. Many people travel from around the world to train with us – just as I did years ago when I trained with my trainer of choice.

We have between 6-8 training intakes per year and allow a maximum of 20 participants in any training. Because of the limited space, we encourage you to secure your seat in the training as soon as you can, even if the trainign that fits your schedule is many months in the future.

Once you enrol, we will get you set up with one of our Transformation Team for a call to do your Onboarding; you'll get set up with your login to the Student Membership Site where you can get started on the pre-course learning tools, which will allow you to use your NLP skills immediately.

Your learning with NLP Worldwide has already started, and we offer our ongoing learning opportunities to you forever. You will have lifetime access to the Student Membership site, which is updated regularly with new articiles, tips, insights and reminders about NLP. You can review any of the NLP trainings for free or for a very minimal cost. We believe that you are in charge of your learning and offer a variety of ways to stay involved, continue learning and being a part of the NLP Coaching community as much or as little as you wish.

So, the only question is – when can we chat?

We are looking forward to sharing more of our world of NLP with you soon.

# RESOURCES

There is a lot that you can start to learn about NLP, so I wanted to make sure I leave you with a variety of resources that will help you to know more and make a very well formed decision about where you go from here.

The following resources are aimed at helping you to know more about NLP and NLP Coaching. Simply click on the image on the left and you'll be transported to the correct place to access the resources!

For now, best of luck in your research and future endeavours! I truly hope I get to meet you in the NLP Training room soon!

## SCHEDULE A SUCCESS CALL

Let's chat. Schedule a call for us to see if this training fits your needs and if you meet what we look for in our Coaches. The call takes about 15-20 minutes, we ask that you have your questions ready and an awareness of why you want to Coach.

## DOWNLOAD THE NLP COACH CERTIFICATION PROSPECTUS

Gain even more information and insight into the program with our course prospectus. Find out the upcoming training dates and start to plan your journey to becoming a Coach.

---

## YOU MUST LEARN NLP – 156 REASONS WHY YOU SHOULD LEARN NLP.

This is a great introduction to NLP book written by Laureli Blyth and me to help you to find out how you will personally benefit from learning NLP.

## 30 DAYS TO NLP

This is the text that we use for our NLP Certification trainings. The book, written by Laureli Blyth  and me provides a simple way to get to know and learn some of the tools and concepts of NLP. E-book $19.95, paperback $42.92 plus postage

## INTRO TO NLP COACHING WEBINAR

Spend 30 minutes online with me learning the ins and outs of the NLP Coach Certification program. This is a great way to see and hear some of the information contained in this book.

# ONLINE COACH DEMONSTRATIONS

Each month we broadcast two Coaching sessions with the same client – an initial client intake and a second session. This gives you the opportunity to see what NLP Coaching looks like and gives you a feel for what it's like to work with others.

# HOW ABOUT NON-NLP COACH TRAINING?

We work closely with the Australian Institute of Professional Coaches, in fact I share a little taste of NLP with their students. Their Coach training is focused more on Positive Psychology and traditional Coaching tools. If this would be more your thing, check their online based Coach training.